UNMASKING THE WOLF
How to Understand Your Dog

By Carolyn Little

Illustrations by: Ziza S (www.orangecupstudio.co.uk)

ISBN 978-1-5272-3944-9

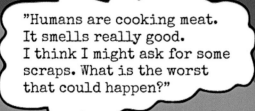

CHAPTERS

"Dog's Are Just Wolves
in Sheep's Clothing"
Stanley Coren
Professor Emeritus

THE WOLF IN YOUR LIVING ROOM
How Wolves Became Dogs

How did a powerful killing machine with awesome weaponry like the wolf turn into a loveable mutt and Man's best friend?

To find the answer we have to go back more than 15,000 years ago deep into our evolutionary past. At this point in time climate shift had altered our ancestors' nomadic way of life and they started to settle into permanent hunter gatherer societies. They started to farm and created garbage dumps. The wolf, ever the opportunist, started to exploit this new food source. Drawn to human settlements by his extraordinary sense of smell, the less fearful wolves approached nearer and nearer to humans and, over thousands of years, evolutionary change took place. The resulting prototype dog became genetically diverse from his wild wolf cousins. This was the start of a symbiotic partnership and the deep bond between man and dog.

The fossil record shows proof of this close relationship. Burial sites have been discovered in Germany, Palestine, Czech Republic and, more recently, Belgium, that have been carbon dated possibly back to 100,000 years. Cave paintings in the early Neolithic period depict Man and wolf hunting together. Paintings in Laas Gaal, Somalia show dogs with humans and caves at Chauvet show paw prints and a child's footprints side by side. It is thought that domestication occurred at different sites at different times.

Because the wolves that approached the early settlements and ate in the presence of humans showed traits of friendliness, tameness and playfulness these juvenile ontogenetic traits were naturally selected for over time and the morphology of the animal changed. Their motor patterns altered. They were no longer in a primitive threatening environment and they no longer needed the advanced cognitive and sensory abilities or ferocity of their wolf ancestors. Their skull size altered, their teeth became smaller and certain behaviours changed or reduced such as regurgitation of food for their young and the motor patterns of stalk, grab, kill and dissect. Instead of having to make life and death decisions on a daily basis to ensure their survival they started to look to humans for help.

Research by Axelsson comparing dog and wolf mDNA, focussed on AMY2B, a gene that codes for starch absorption. He found that dog saliva contains more amylase enzymes which suggest that the dog's digestion evolved to digest the starchier food found at human garbage dumps compared with the carnivorous diet of the wolf.

Studies also suggest that traits in the dog show them to be more sociable, less fearful and more able to read our behavioural cues. In fact, behaviourally, we humans are more similar to dogs than our closest primate cousins. Further research centred on ancient burial sites in Siberia and modern-day canids. This identified the gene (SLC6A4) that controls neuronal uptake of serotonin, the "feelgood" hormone. This is the neurotransmitter that affects "tameness" This behavioural change suggests the genomic shift was able to modify the innate hardwired behaviour of ferocious predation and produce our much-loved canine companions.

The extreme differentiation in dogs that we see today came about mainly in the last two centuries when selective breeding became fashionable. Today we see the Chihuahua and the Great Dane sitting side by side — at great morphological distance and we know that they share the same chromosomes and that they are both descended from the Wolf.

The dog will always have one paw in the past.

Developmental Stages of the Dog

Pre - natal Period

This is the time before birth when the pup is safely in his mother's womb. It is thought that stress hormones, adrenaline and cortisol, circulating in the maternal blood stream could be damaging to the foetus and affect the puppy's future physiological reactions to stress. It is therefore important to make sure the bitch is well looked after and avoids unnecessary stress during pregnancy.

Neonatal - Birth to 2 Weeks

Puppies are born blind and deaf with very little ability to move. They cannot regulate their temperature so they huddle together for warmth. They are totally dependent on their mothers for basic survival. They suckle milk and obtain some antibodies from colostrum. The mother encourages them to defaecate by ano-genital licking. They have some response to touch. It is beneficial for them to be gently handled by humans at this stage so that the process of imprinting on humans begins.

Transitional Period – 2 to 3 Weeks

This is when their eyes open and they startle to sudden noise (the auditory startle response). This is a basic evolutionary survival mechanism enabling them to recognise danger and habituate to their environment. Baby teeth erupt and they are ready to be weaned. The puppies begin to void without help from their mother. They start to crawl and explore their environment. They learn important lessons from their mother and litter mates at this stage such as bite inhibition. This is a vital period for learning. At this stage they start exhibiting behaviours and displaying social signals. They start play fighting with their litter mates, test their hunting skills and explore their surroundings.

The Window of Opportunity When Important Learning Takes Place

Socialisation Period
— 3 weeks to 12 weeks

This is a critical period for a puppy and if the right lessons are not learned it will have an impact on his entire life. Their brains are developing rapidly in terms of neuronal connections, imprinting takes place and they start to understand their identity as a dog. Attachments are formed to both people and places. It is a vital developmental window in which specific experiences can have irreversible effects on behaviour leading to fear and aggression, inability to socialise with other dogs, dislike or fear of children, large men, bicycles, fireworks etc. It is important for them to have positive experiences at this stage and have contact with new things and different people in a safe environment and to avoid any frightening experiences which could impact on the puppy's mental development. At this stage they are going through the first fear period when they become hypersensitive to stress. It is important to protect them from harmful experiences. The effects of bad experiences can last a lifetime and lead to phobias and a nervous emotionally unstable dog.

Juvenile Period 10 months to 2 years

These are the teenage years when the wolf heritage may well emerge. The puppy might try to assert dominance over family, resource guard and rebel against rules and boundaries. The baby teeth fall out and the adult teeth erupt. They get their thick adult coat and become sexually mature. However emotionally and mentally they are still a puppy. It is thought that around this time a second fear period occurs and again it is important they feel safe and secure.

Old Age

Just as with people, dogs may start to lose some of their cognitive faculties. If there is hearing loss it it might help to stomp on the floor so he knows you are coming and talk to him more to let him know you are around. He might need medication for painful joints. This all helps to manage the situation.

Wolf cubs form a tight family pack and don't like strangers whereas puppies form strong attachments to humans.

Wolves enter the development stages sooner than puppies. They start exploring their surroundings before their eyes are fully open.

Wolves enter the critical period two weeks earlier than dogs. Like puppies they play with their littermates and practice their hunting skills. They like to stalk, and pounce. At 3 weeks they eat meat regurgitated by their mother. In the socialisation period they learn to play fight and assert dominance. Wolf pups are learning to kill whereas puppies rely on us for food.

At **4 – 8 months wolf cubs** join the adults on hunting trips and learn to ambush and kill as a team.
At **9 - 12 months wolf cubs** mark and monitor their territory.

Being a dog – living in a world beyond human eyes

Dogs live in a world that is largely closed to humans. Like us, they interpret their environment through auditory, olfactory and visual cues but they are anatomically and behaviourally different from us. They have adapted to the human environment through natural evolutionary and artificial selective pressures but have retained much of their superior lupine qualities. These traits enabled them to survive and reproduce in their ancestral world and to guard their territories. Dogs have superior sensory and perceptual systems to us and it is this that underpins their bond with humans and has ensured their success in the modern world.

Hearing

Dog, like wolves, have excellent hearing which is greatly superior to that of humans. This enables them to hear sounds that we cannot.

They have ears which are anatomically and structurally similar to ours consisting of four parts:

- the highly mobile and vascular pinna,
- the external auditory meatus lined with sebaceous and apocrine glands,
- the middle ear and
- the inner ear.

The eardrum separates the external ear from the middle ear. The middle ear contains three bones, the malleus, the stapes and the incus, that transmit vibrations to the inner ear. This consists of the cochlear and semi-circular canals which are also involved in balance. In the cochlea specialised cells and cilia transmit signals along the auditory nerve to the auditory cortex in the brain where it is interpreted as sound.

The pinna in dogs has eighteen muscles enabling them to more easily locate the direction of sounds. Primates (including humans) have largely lost this ability over the course of evolution. By moving their outer ears and noting the difference in sound waves arriving at the left and right ears the dog's brain is able to triangulate and compute the sound direction.

The position of the dog's ears reflects his mood and this is something that humans and other dogs can read. Unfortunately artificial selection has in some breeds reduced the dog's ability to signal.

Dogs are able to **hear ultrasound frequencies** above the human threshold of 20 KHz. It is thought they can hear up to 80 KHz. This is an important adaptation as it enabled their ancestors to hear the high sounds of vermin and rodents which once were part of their diet. It enables wolves to locate exact position of prey and to hear the approach of other predators at a distance. This ability to hear high sounds is why some dogs like to play with squeaky toys.

Puppies are born deaf and their ears open at around four weeks. They convey distress calls to their mothers via ultrasound. Some rodents and bats communicate by ultrasound and this is why dogs seem to hear things that we cannot.

Dogs and wolves have the **ability to filter out unimportant stimuli**. This is an important skill in the Wild where a wolf only needs to pay attention to what affects his survival. That is why a dog can ignore conversation but jump up when he hears the word "Walk."

Because the larynx is longer in larger animals, dogs are able to assess the size of another dog in the neighbourhood from the bark sound. Congenital deafness is sometimes present in some breeds often associated with the merle or piebald gene (i.e. Dalmatians, Australian shepherds, bull terrier etc.) These dogs respond better to visual signals.

Vision

A dog's eyes are anatomically different from humans. We have trichromatic vision which means we have three cones enabling us to see red and green and blue. Dogs have dichromatic vision and only have two cones meaning they can only distinguish colour in a narrower range. They see yellow and blue and shades of grey.

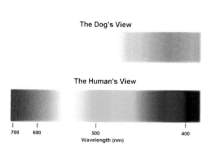

Colour vision is not vital for survival when hunting in low light and wolves depend more on their powers of smell and hearing. Unlike primates they don't need to hunt out sweet red fruit. That's why a dog can't always see a red ball on a green lawn.

Otherwise their eyes are **structurally and functionally** similar to us although humans have a fovea which dogs do not. The dog's eye consists of two fluid filled chambers separated by the lens. The pupil is surrounded by the iris which has muscles attached which contract to open and close the lens and let in more light. Light enters through the pupil and passes onto the light sensitive cells of the retina which transmit signals along the optic nerve to the brain where it is interpreted. The retina is lined with rods and cones. In dogs the lens is bigger than humans is and closer to the retina making the image brighter.

Dogs have a **wider field of vision** depending on breed. They have a 250 degree field of vision as opposed to 180 in humans. This is an adaptation enabling them to hunt and at the same time be wary of predators on the periphery of their field of vision.

Humans have evolved as a **diurnal species** whereas wolves hunt at night or early morning when the prey comes out to forage. Dogs have adapted to our daily rhythms but they are a nocturnal, crepuscular species and tend to be more active at these times. They do not see as well as us in low light but the tapetum, an extra layer of light reflective cells, is able to mirror light. Dogs' eyes are adapted to detect movement and it is this that triggers the prey instinct. They are sensitive to a higher flicker rate than humans and this is why dogs don't watch much television.

The ability to make **eye contact** with humans has secured a dog's place in the human world and strengthened the bond between the two species. Unlike dogs, wolves do not initiate the oxytocin feedback loop with humans

Sense of Smell

Dogs have extraordinary olfactory capabilities. For most breeds smell is their primary sense and the means by which they interpret the world around them and recognise individuals. The area of a dogs' brain devoted to olfaction is approximately forty times that of humans. We have five million olfactory receptors. They have two hundred and fifty million. This amazing ability comes from their ancestral behaviour of territoriality and predation.

Their noses are anatomically different from humans. We smell and breathe through the same airways but in dogs these functions are separate. A dog sniffs and draws in air through his mobile nostrils which act independently. Air enters his nose where the flow is divided by a flap of tissue called the septum. Some air goes to his lungs where gaseous exchange takes place. The rest is drawn by cilia over the mucosal epithelial lining of the turbinate bones where molecules of scent are absorbed and picked up by receptors cells. These are then sent via neural circuitry to the olfactory centre in the brain where it is analysed by each component. Where we smell stew, dogs smell meat, potatoes, herbs etc.

Air is exhaled through slits in the sides of their nose enabling dogs to breathe and sniff at the same time.

Dogs have a secondary sensory system located behind the incisors. This is known as the Jacobson or vomeronasal organ and enables the dog to detect a pheromonal profile of friend or foe. Pheromones are species specific chemicals released from the dog's ears, interdigital, genito-anal area and mammary sulci. They play an important role in survival and reproduction by generating appropriate behavioural responses. They are taken in through the nose and, bypassing the hypothalamus, connect directly to the limbic system – the emotional centre of the brain. The dog is able to assess gender, age and reproductive status. Dogs can locate a female in season by smell and it is the methyl hydro benzoate in urine that triggers mounting behaviour.

When humans are stressed a cascade of catecholamines is released into the blood stream including adrenaline, dopamine and cortisol. Dogs smell this in the sweat from our apocrine glands and are able to judge our mood from this and our facial expression and body language. That is why they look stressed and seemingly guilty when we come home and get angry on seeing a raid on the dustbin. Dogs smell fear and anger. They can also be trained to smell an epileptic aura and hypoglycaemia.

Smell is involved in the ancestral wolf behaviours of territoriality, predation, mating and reproduction. This is why dogs urinate on lamp posts to leave their signature and let the neighbourhood know who they are and what they are about.

The wolf uses his sense of smell to locate prey and, it is thought that he avoids predators, by disguising his own scent. This is thought to be vestigial hunting behaviour in dogs and why it is difficult to stop them rolling in something smelly.

Wolves and dogs have a sense of smell one hundred times better than humans. A wolf can smell prey more than 1.7 miles away. They both use their superior sense of smell to navigate the world. Smell is a primary sense for most dogs enabling to identify individuals by gender, reproductive status and mood. The pheromones they release can identify another animal with the accuracy of a human finger print. The also like to leave their own smell by urinating to mark the boundaries of their territory and to make their surroundings familiar.

Dogs have adapted over thousands of years to they thrive in the modern human world but they still retain many of their superior lupine faculties that enabled their ancestors to be a top predator of the Ice Age.

Is it any wonder dogs pull on the lead. They want to be off exploring a secret world that is closed to humans.

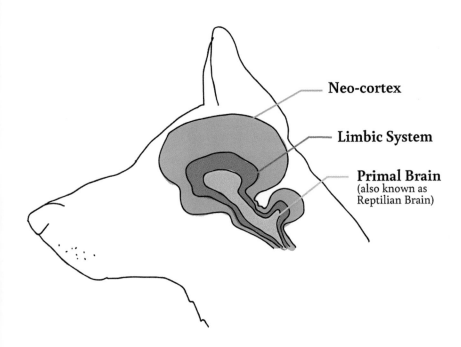

The brain consists of three parts:

The Primal Brain (also known as the Reptilian Brain)

This is the ancient first part of the brain that evolved from basic life forms. It is rigid and compulsive. It contains basic reflexes and controls routines and the basic survival functions of breathing, eating, sleeping, mating, tribalism and territoriality. It responds to danger by the fear response (flight, fight or freeze via the Amygdala) or anger display. It locates females in heat and recognises friend and foe. That's why rituals are important to the primal brain. It makes wolves, dogs and humans feel safe.

The Limbic System

This is the emotional centre of the brain that makes value judgements and leads to social learning. It is hardwired to remember a negative emotional experience to ensure the future safety of the animal. It contains the dopaminergic motivational systems and understands the concept of reward. It records memories of events both good and bad. Emotions directly affect behaviour and this is the part of the canine brain we need to tap into during training.

The Neo-cortex

This is the most recently evolved part of the brain which controls rational thinking, problem solving and decision making. The neo-cortex can be knocked offline when a dog is overwhelmed by fear or stress and that's when he forgets his training.

All three areas of the brain are interconnected but wolves have far more problem solving abilities than dogs. The wolf brain is larger than that of a dog. It is two thirds of comparable body size. Wolves have to be constantly alert and make life or death decisions on a daily basis.

Humans and dogs have evolved alongside each other and our brains are similar.

> Dogs will always look to us for guidance

FLIGHT, FIGHT OR FREEZE
An Ancient Survival Mechanism

Freeze

Flee

4xF

Fight

Fidget about

Fear lies at the heart of most canine behavioural problems. It is the most powerful primal emotion a dog has and is designed to protect the animal against predators. If he cannot take flight or freeze then he will turn to aggression to defend himself against a real or perceived threat.

Sensory information enters the dog's brain via the Amygdala. This is on permanent guard against threats and acts as an early warning system to alert the animal to danger and prepare him for action either to flee, freeze or fight. The behaviour is hardwired into the animal and is part an evolutionary defence mechanism for survival to enable him for to protect himself. Wolves are more aggressive than dogs and need to be constantly alert against predators in the Wild. They will use ritualised postures and behaviour to defuse situations but will kill if necessary. Dogs are more likely to be fearful and look to us for help.

When the Amygdala is triggered it acts on the hypothalamic adreno pituitary axis which uses the blood stream and the nervous system to release a cascade of catecholamines such as noradrenaline, dopamine, acetylcholine, adrenaline serotonin etc. These hormones ready us for action and put us all, wolf, dog and human into a state of flight, freeze or fight. Body systems are shut down except those needed for defence or attack. Heart rate and blood pressure increases to bring more oxygen to the muscles, hackles are raised to make the animal appear bigger and more threatening, eyes dilate to take in more light to fixate on the target, respiration increases and digestion shuts down. Dogs sometimes involuntarily urinate. The rational thinking part of a dog's brain goes off line completely and he won't respond to what the owner says. His reaction is the same whether it's a lion or next door's cat. The Amygdala cannot distinguish between a real threat or a false alarm. It creates a memory of a fearful experience and this is what can leads to phobias in dogs.

This is why it is so important to gently introduce a puppy to new experiences. This makes him robust and resilient as an adult and able to cope with new situations without panicking.

Never try to get a dog to confront his fears. Avoid anything stressful and introduce new things very slowly.

Oxytocin – the Love Hormone, the Ancient Bond

The most important training tool is the bond that exists between dog and human. This bond is mediated by the hormone oxytocin. When we stare into their eyes and they stare back it creates a feedback loop. This is the hormone that bonds mother and newborn child and bonds humans to their dogs. It's the hormone that makes humans fall in love.

Wild wolves don't make eye contact with humans. They see it as an aggressive challenge. We share an oxytocin feedback loop with dogs not with wolves.

Oxytocin is responsible for social bonding. Wolves are successful at hunting because they are able to bond with the pack and cooperate to kill prey. Dogs bond with us and want to please us.

Dogs share a closer relationship with us than any other animal due to their unique cognitive abilities and ability to bond with us. This is a bi- product of their selection for tameness.

Oxytocin is the mysterious alchemy between dog and human and the reason why dogs steal our hearts

Adrenaline

Adrenaline and noradrenaline are secreted by the adrenal glands and prepare the body for action in an emergency situation. Wolves by their nature are reactive and aggressive and in the Wild have to be on constant alert for danger. They need this aggression to fuel their predatory instincts and kill their food. Co-evolution and selective pressure has rewired the genomes of both wolf and dog. Dogs have reduced genes that code for adrenaline and domestication has removed much of their predatory instincts. They bond with us. They have much less aggression as humans provide for their needs but too much adrenaline will still put them in survival mode and lead to over reactivity. That's why we need to provide them with a calm, stress free environment.

Dopamine – The Natural High

This is the powerful reward hormone which causes humans to become addicted to gambling or heroin. We get that same rush of pleasure when we achieve something. That's how a dog feels when he does what we want and we reward him with praise or chicken. Dopamine leads to feelings of overwhelming pleasure. It's the hormone that gives us motivation and anticipation of reward is a powerful learning tool.

Endorphins

These are naturally occurring, calming opiates produced in the brains of wolves and dogs and released during play, exercise and social bonding. Adult wolves rarely play but wolf cubs use play to learn hunting skills. Dogs love play just for the fun of it and it binds them to their humans. It's good for dogs and humans. That's why dogs find human interaction rewarding in itself.

Cortisol

Cortisol is released when a dog is stressed. It helps him cope with a worrying situation. It is longer lasting than adrenaline and too much can cause long term damage.

Cortisol is a stress hormone that prepares the animal for danger.

A high cortisol level overwhelms the brain and knocks out rational thought.

Adrenaline can sometimes be useful as it sharpens reactions but continued stress can lead to over production of cortisol which will have a damaging effect on behaviour and health. Dogs have much lower levels of these hormones because they look to us to problem solve and meet their survival needs. When cortisol and adrenaline are constantly released it puts a dog in a constant state of stress.

Dogs don't always need their ancestral wolf skills they've got us to help them adjust to the world they live in.

A Happy and Relaxed Dog

Worried Dog who feels uncomfortable and wants to be left alone

> If a dog is anxious he forgets his training and cannot think his way out of a problem.

Serotonin - the Feel Good Hormone

Serotonin regulates mood and promotes friendliness and bonding. Increased levels of serotonin lead to feelings of well - being and happiness. Low levels lead to depression and anxiety in humans.

Wolves and dogs have different brain chemistry. There is a genetic difference in the gene that codes for serotonin. Dogs are usually calm and happy whereas wolves are aggressive and reactive. Selection for tameness resulted in alteration of the serotonergic pathway in wolf and prototype dog.

Back in the Pleistene Ice Age it made sense for the two top predators, wolf and human to be nice to each other, to avoid conflict and cooperate in hunting. Early life for Man was brutal. It was kill or be killed and when man and wolf joined forces they made a formidable hunting team. During a period of co-evolution the SLc 6A4 gene that codes for serotonin was selected and living in a shared environment was the driver of genetic change making early Man and proto dog less aggressive.

Now wolves live peaceably within the pack but still retain their high levels of aggression for when they need to fight, flee or kill.
Co- evolution and selective pressure has rewired the genomes of both dogs and wolves.

Oestradiol, Progesterone and Luteinizing Hormones

Female wolves and dogs have similar endocrine profiles which cause behaviour change. In wolves hormones cycle to allow cubs to be born in Spring to give them the best chance of survival. Dogs usually have 2 cycles per year.

Wolves and dogs have a sense of smell one hundred times better than humans. A wolf can smell prey more than 1.7 miles away. They both use their superior sense of smell to navigate the world. Smell is a primary sense for most dogs enabling to identify individuals by gender, reproductive status and mood. The pheromones they release can identify another animal with the accuracy of a human finger print.

The also like to leave their own smell by urinating to mark the boundaries of their territory and to make their surroundings familiar.

INSTINCTS, DRIVES AND MOTIVATIONS OF WOLVES AND DOGS

Recognising the primal instincts that motivate the wolf is the key to understanding canine behaviour.

Instincts and drives arising in the ancient part of the brain are hardwired into wolves enabling them to survive in the Wild. These are:

Territoriality

Wolves live in clearly defined territories. They are suspicious of strangers on their borders and will howl to alert pack members. They have developed complex rituals of body language to defuse aggression and deter intruders but if that doesn't work they will fight to kill. Dogs retain this guarding instinct but will bark to alert humans.

Ask a dog to guard your house but don't ask him to guard your dinner – the lupine instincts will kick in.

Sex Drive and Mating Instinct

This is to preserve the species. In wolves only the alphas (the breeding pair) have breeding rights. Dogs have no such hierarchy. They live in the human pack and breed randomly if not neutered.

Maternal Instinct

Both wolves and dogs nurture and fiercely protect their young. Their behaviour is driven by hormones.

Cacheing Food

Wolves live in harsh conditions and bury surplus from the kill to eat later. Dogs dig in the garden and bury bones.

Pack Instinct

Wolves are highly social animals and like to live in a pack. The wolf pack motto is **"Together We Are Strong."** They will howl to keep in contact with each other. Dogs like to be in the human pack and be part of the family. They don't like to spend long on their own.

Prey Instinct

Wolves have a complex prey drive involving seeking, hunting, retrieving, chasing, stalking, pouncing, shaking, grabbing, bite and kill. These are genetically driven instincts fuelled by high adrenaline enabling them to survive and reproduce in the Wild. Fortunately in domestic dogs this is diminished and truncated but we can still see the residual sequence in play. That's why dogs love a game of tug.

When dealing with problem behaviours such as digging up the garden, chewing carpets, separation anxiety, growling at strange dogs, rummaging in dustbins, barking, chasing cats we need to recognise the instincts and drives that come from their lupine ancestry but remember

Wolves have a killer instinct
- dogs do not

Wolves live peaceably in a pack under complex rules of behaviour. They have a sophisticated system of communication involving body language, vocalisation, smells and pheromones. Our dogs have adapted to live happily with us in the human pack. They read our signals and we need to learn to read theirs so we can be aware of their emotional state.

Both dogs and wolves need social interaction in order to thrive. Wolves live and work together to hunt, establish territories and raise pups. Dogs meet their social and other needs with humans and they form strong attachments with us. When given a puzzle to solve dogs look to us for guidance but wolves will try to solve it on their own. Dogs can read human gestures and follow our gaze wolves cannot. Dogs are direct descendants of the Grey Wolf and share 98% of genes. They have common behaviours and physical attributes but selection for "tameness" has distorted the genetic make up and led to changes in the fight or flight biochemical pathway. The behaviours we value in dogs today are the basis of what wolves do to survive in the Wild. Dogs have less adrenaline response than wolves and this makes them more receptive to training by us. However remnants of the wolf ancestry remain in our dogs.

Dogs like wolves communicate with body language, pheromones, vocalisations and action signals. Always watch the signals to be aware of the body language of your dog. Dogs are adept at picking up human signals. They can tune into our emotions and form an abstract mental representation. It is this unique ability that has driven domestication and enabled them to live alongside us and form powerful bonds.

Wolves and Dogs are genetically programmed to regard strangers with suspicion but from about six weeks they learn the signals of an elaborate greeting ritual and are able to assess the other animal and avoid conflict. Wolves will not usually tolerate individuals from other packs but dogs generally want to be friends with other dogs.

When two dogs meet each other messages are exchanged at a chemical level. These are mainly pheromones that are secreted in the ears, lips and in the interdigital, urogenital and anal areas. The ritual of sniffing each other is part of a species specific etiquette where the dogs gather valuable information about each other with regard to gender, status, reproductive state, mood and intent. The superior scent organs in the dog's nose gather up the scent molecules and send it to the brain to be interpreted. Decisions to act are made in seconds.

Body Language

Dogs and wolves send, receive and interpret information and formulate responses through their body language. They communicate their emotions through different parts of their body, ears, facial expression, tail, eyes, body carriage, position and posture. They are adept at reading our body language and we need to learn to read their bodily cues in order to accurately interpret them and understand them so that we can meet their needs and strengthen the bond between dog and human.

When training it is useful to remember that dogs register visual signals more than auditory ones so it is a good idea to add in hand signals.

The main behaviours of dogs reflect those of wolves in regard to social interaction, feeding, reproduction and they retain the remnants of predatory and hunting behaviours. They display emotional states of fear, distress, aggression and "playfulness" and "happiness."

Much of dog's language comes from the ancestral lupine heritage when complex body signals evolved to reduce conflict. It is rare for fights to take place in the wolf pack as ritualised threat displays are used to reduce aggression and maintain hierarchy. In the same way dogs use subtle social and appeasement signals to avoid fights.
Wolves engage in aggressive rituals on the borders of their territory to deter intruders from another pack. If that doesn't work they launch savage attacks.

Dogs will always negotiate for the best outcome.

Learn to read the signals

I want to play. Wolf cubs love to play but rarely play as adults.

Dogs of any age love to play.

Dogs love a tug game

Lip licking means he's very uncomfortable with what is going on.

This dog is very stressed and trying to appease its owner.

This dog is alert and anxious. Not sure what to do.

Don't be cross with me.

I'm really scared

What's going on?
I'm suspicious

Passive
Submission

Active
Submission

Happy relaxed
confident dog

Aggresive attack

Dogs communicate by **growling and barking**. Adult wolves rarely bark but howl to communicate with the pack. Humans selected dogs with loud barks to warn them of intruders and protect their camps so don't blame a dog for barking.

A dog who is confident and alert will have his ears erect and forward facing. An anxious, submissive dog will hold his ears back and, if fearful, flat to his head.

Attentive

Appeasing

Fearful Anxious

Relaxed

The tail is a powerful communicator and will be held high in an alert, confident dog, slightly lower when relaxed, stiff in an aggressive dog and low and tucked in a submissive or fearful dog. A hooked tail could mean frustration.

Wagging usually means friendliness but a slow twitch could be the start of aggression so it is important to be aware of conflicting emotions in a dog.

The mouth of an aggressive dog will be open in a C shape to show his full weaponry whereas a friendly dog will have a relaxed half open mouth probably with his tongue showing. A fearful dog will have his lips closed and tight.

Unfortunately selective breeding by humans has meant some breeds of dogs have reduced signalling ability.

Learn to read your dog's body language so you read his mood.

Their unique abilities to communicate have enabled them to adapt to our world, and to live alongside us.

Aggression towards other dogs is almost always fear based. It is very, very unlikely to lead to a biting attack but you do need to be aware what's going on with him.

Dominance / Aggression
(Offensive threat)

Ears Forward

Wrinkled nose and forehead

Hackles raised

Lips curled

Teeth and gums showing

Tail raised, stiff, bristled

Mouth open

Legs stiff

Leaning forward

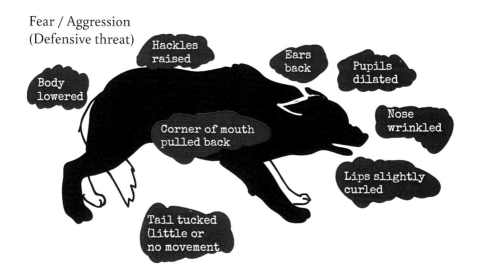

Fear / Aggression
(Defensive threat)

Hackles raised

Ears back

Pupils dilated

Body lowered

Nose wrinkled

Corner of mouth pulled back

Lips slightly curled

Tail tucked (little or no movement

The reason he doesn't like other dogs is because he's frightened of them and feels uneasy around them. He was possibly poorly socialised when he was a puppy and now he can't read their signals and he feels threatened. Try not to put him in a situation that makes him feel uncomfortable and that he can't cope with. He sees other dogs as a threat and probably feels he has to protect you.
When you walk him be alert to other dogs and be prepared to take avoiding action. Try to block his view of the other dog and turn away. Try to get his attention on you and put some distance between you and the other dog. Don't yank on his collar or he will get more frustrated.

The best thing you could do is buy a **head collar**. They go by the brand name of Halti or Gentle Leader. That way you can gently get control of his head and get him to look at you and then speak to him in a reassuring way. Whatever happens don't get angry or shout because that will make him more nervous. If he stays calm and you get past the other dog reward him with praise and a treat. That way he will realise that seeing other dogs is a pleasant experience not a frightening one. If he's a nervous dog you might find he's suspicious of the head collar because its something new so make sure you introduce it slowly and lure him into it with treats.

The best thing you could do would be to try to find someone who has got a really docile friendly dog and go out walking with them. Walk the dogs at distance a few yards apart to start with and then gradually decrease the distance and keep the rewards going when he stays calm. If he can relax with one dog then he might generalise it to other dogs and you might be able to take him to a dog class but take things slowly because it will take him a very long time for him to feel completely unthreatened and relaxed around other dogs.

It goes without saying that a nervous dog needs a lot of security and reassurance and a strict routine of walks, different environments to sniff round and toys to keep him occupied.

Dog behaviour
is either:

A)

hardwired into the animal as a result of evolutionary adaptations or selective breeding and is part of the dog's genetic blue print originating from the wolf. It is often breed specific i.e. guarding, swimming, herding. It is difficult to alter basic drives and motor patterns because these are natural behaviours and this is what it means to be a dog.

or:

B)

it is learnt as a result of training and environment. What they learn during the socialisation period of their puppy lives is critically important. Positive experiences in this time results in a happy well balanced dog.

43

Observational Learning

This is where puppies learn the important cues of dog life such as signals, body language and behaviours from other dogs. These behavioural cues are universal in dog communication and this is why it is vital to socialise a puppy with other dogs. Unfortunately some breeding programmes have reduced visual signals in some dogs.

Habituation

This is where a dog gets used to something that is introduced into his environment as a neutral stimulus. He has not seen it before and it has neither high or low salience for him for him so he will learn to ignore it.

Genetics plays a part in this. Some dogs are curious and bold, others are more fearful. By being exposed to new stimuli in a non-threatening environment the dog learns to ignore them. This forms the basis of a calm, predictable dog. That is why it is important to introduce a puppy to a wide variety of stimuli, such as traffic, children, noises, people in hats etc. and they will learn to accept them. Wolf cubs cannot be tamed but if they are introduced to humans during the critical period (first fear stage) they will accept them.

Sensitisation

This is where a dog is fearful of loud fireworks or other frightening experiences. This fear gradually increases and extends to all loud noises. This is known as generalisation. The response increases over time (i.e. cowering, shivering, hiding, and barking) and November the 5th becomes a nightmare. This is why it is essential to introduce a puppy to unusual noise or objects in the socialisation period.

Operant Conditioning

This is associative learning by trial and error. It is a form of learning where behaviour is modified by consequences both positive and negative

The puppy learns A
If I sit then B. happens.
I get praise or a treat.

And
If he A chases next door's cat he might B get a scratch.

Wolves adapt their behaviour and survive by learning what benefits them and what doesn't. They weigh up the cost benefit of their decisions and act accordingly.

It is always a good idea to find out what your dog is really motivated by. His favourite reward might be chicken or cheese, a game with his favourite toy or often, best of all, praise from his owner.

Classical Conditioning

This helps a dog make a specific association with a specific stimulus. i.e. the owner puts his shoes on and gets out the lead, the dog knows he's going for a walk so gets excited, jumps up and down and wags his tail.

If he is fearful, pair the stimulus with a positive. If he doesn't like his teeth cleaned give a treat when the toothbrush is produced.

Desensitisation and Counter Conditioning

This is where we try to alter the dog's emotional response to a previously conditioned response by reducing his response and pairing it with a new response.

Reduction of a Dog's Response to Stimuli – Loud Fireworks/Household Appliances

This means exposing the dog to his fear very, very gradually and replacing a negative emotional state with a positive reinforcer (a treat, games etc.).

For example if the dog has a fear of fireworks play a DVD of fireworks or other sounds at increasing intensity over a period of weeks at times when he feels safe and is being given treats or playing games. Play it quietly over a smart phone when he is out enjoying his walk and gradually he will become conditioned to make positive association, lose his fear and stop reacting.

How to teach a dog to sit:

The most important training tool is the bond between human and dog. It is usually easy to train them because they want to please us and they are adept at reading our signals and emotions. Use a gentle happy voice and make training enjoyable and fun. Get him to focus on you and give clear cues both visual and vocal. Show him what to do and give treats and praise the instant he does what he's asked.

Keep training sessions very short and never, never get impatient or angry, just try again another day. Remember dogs can't always generalise so what he learns in the living room needs to be proofed in the kitchen, the bedroom, the hall, the garden and on a walk. Train in a calm pleasant environment when both you and he are in a relaxed happy mood. **(Serotonin)**

Get him to look at you using" look at me" cue and pointing to your eyes. **(Oxytocin)**

Repeat the word "sit" and use a treat as a lure.

As soon as he sits say the words "sit", "good boy" and give him the treat **(Dopamine)** That way you "capture" the behaviour.
He starts to understand that if I sit when I'm told to **I get** a treat. (Operant Conditioning)

Training is fun because I get treats and praise (Classical Conditioning).

When he's repeated the behaviour a few times start giving random rewards. This is a very powerful technique as it taps into the "gambling centres" of the brain. It is the unpredictability of a win that makes humans buy lottery tickets. The mere thought of a win causes neurons in the brain to produce dopamine and this gives motivation and satisfaction. The dog doesn't know when the treat is coming so he tries harder and stays alert.

Make training fun

Dogs in Society

The relationship between man and dog is a special one and the strong bond between us has led to dogs playing astonishing roles in society. Different breeds are selected for different tasks.
Here are just a few examples of Man's dependence on the superior physical and cognitive powers of dogs.

Guide Dogs

Dogs have a long history of helping people dating back to early Man when dogs and humans formed a partnership to track and kill prey for food.

A 16th Century children's poem records "A was an Archer/and shot at a frog/B was a blind man led by a dog.

Today there are over 4800 highly trained guide dogs in the UK and they have been able to transform the lives of blind and partially sighted people.

German Shepherds and Labrador retrievers are usually selected for this work as they have the calm happy temperament necessary for this important role.

Guide dogs have a long and expensive training.
They are trained to:

- Work as a team with the handler.
- Walk in a straight line.
- Turn left and right and avoid obstacles.
- Wait at curbs
- Take the handler to regular destinations
- And most important of all to know when to disobey a command ie when told to cross a road but they can see a car coming.

They go to a puppy walker's home at six weeks. There they are introduced to the sights and sounds of our complex world and taught basic commands. At 17 months they go back to the Guide Dog Centre to start serious training for the responsible job they will now undertake. Then, after graduation at 22 months, they start their new life as a valued friend, guide and companion.
Of course as with most jobs there will be plenty of downtime for running around and dog fun.

Sniffer Dogs - Dogs Solving Crime

These dogs have access to
a world that is closed to us
— the world of complex smells. They have
over 200 million olfactory cells in their
noses compared to 2 million in ours.
Rather surprisingly cats have even more
but the feline temperament precludes
them from cooperating
with us.

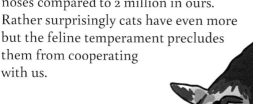

Dogs are used to sniff out substances that humans cannot. They are used to sniff out explosives, blood, cash, and narcotics, even illicit mobile phones in prisons, computer hard drives and bumblebee colonies in conservation projects.

In cases of suspicious fire, they can find traces of accelerant and pinpoint the exact location where the fire was set. They help the police track criminals by smelling sweat particles in the air. They are trained to track ground scents and air scents. Weather conditions make little difference to them as they can follow a trail through blizzards and at night. Most impressive of all they can detect smells under water. These dogs need to have very special skills such as the ability to think and problem solve when out of sight of the handler. The elite squad are the cadaver dogs who are specially trained to sniff out human decomposition in homicide cases. In training, the Police use pork which has a similar composition to human flesh. The dogs are even able to find the exact spot where a murder took place and where the body was stored (ie in the boot of a car.)

These highly trained canines were used in the Tsunami Disaster in Asia, in the 7/7 terrorist attacks in London, the Mudslide disaster in New York and numerous high profile murders. In Nottingham Police dogs Jack and Charley found the burial site of two victims (the Wycherleys) of a 15 year old homicide. Dog handlers are frequently called to court to give evidence.

In spite of numerous attempts to build a machine that mimics a dog's nose no-one has succeeded in doing so.

Sled Dogs

Sled Dogs are powerfully built wolf-like animals that have been used in the icy wastes of the frozen North to transport supplies, rescue casualties and carry mail. Until snow mobiles were invented the only way of crossing the inhospitable terrain was by dog sled. In 1925 when an outbreak of deadly diphtheria broke out in Nome the huskies fulfilled a vital role in transporting vaccine over a thousand miles from Anchorage to save many lives.

Nowadays they are used in sled racing. The dogs are mixed breed selected for performance and strength. They are amazingly strong for their size. They have an inherent drive to pull and they are matched for size and gait within the dog team.

Generations of selective breeding have led to changes that protect them in their environment. They have thick water repellent coats, big bushy tails and paws with adapted sweat glands and fat deposition. They really love the cold preferring it to be below 6 degrees Fahrenheit. They wear bootees to protect their feet against their sweat turning to ice and to protect them against the abrasive action of the snow. They are big eaters and during race days will eat four meals of high fat and protein with treats in between.

These are some of the heroes of the canine world...

In the Wild the wolf lives by the complex rules and rituals of the wolf pack. Dogs share our world and are happy to live by our rules and form bonds with us.

The Dog Owner's Prayer

"Dear Lord, Please make me be the sort of person my dog thinks I am."

Miklosi et al, **A simple reason for a big difference: wolves do not look back at humans, but dogs do**, Current Biology April 29, 2003

Axelsson et al, **The genomic signature of dog domestication reveals adaptation to a starch rich diet.** Nature 2013. 495

Nagasawa et al, **Oxytocin-gaze positive loop and the co-evolution of human-dog bonds**, Science 17th April 2015

Early canid domestication: The Farm-fox experiment
American Scientist 87, 1999

Saetre et al. **From wild wolf to domestic dog: gene expression changes in the brain**, Molecular Brain August 2004 Research 126 (2)

Mech D and Boitani L, **Wolves. Behaviour, Ecology and Conservation**
University of Chicago Press, 2000

Lindsay S, **Handbook of Applied Behaviour and Training** , Blackwell Publishing

Jensen P, **The Behavioural Biology of Dogs**, 2007, Cabi International

Berns G et al, **"Scent of the familiar: An fMRI study of canine brain responses to familiar and unfamiliar human and dog odours."**
Behavioural Processes, Vol 110, Jan 2015, p 37-46